BOOK TWO

The Pleasure Of Your Company

at the playing of

Piano Duets

is requested
by

Melvin Stecher,
Norman Horowitz
& Claire Gordon

ISBN 978-0-7935-7867-2

G. SCHIRMER, Inc.

DISTRIBUTED BY

HAL•LEONARD®
CORPORATION

7777 W. BLUEMOUND RD. P.O. BOX 13819 MILWAUKEE, WI 53213

T0051128

PONY TALES

Secondo

With an easy swing

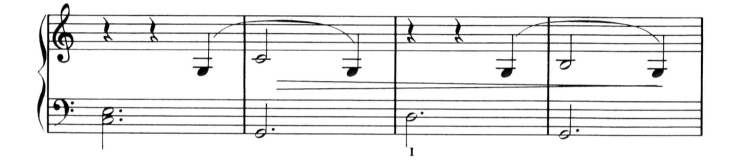

(rit. 2nd time)

Fine

PONY TALES

Primo

With an easy swing

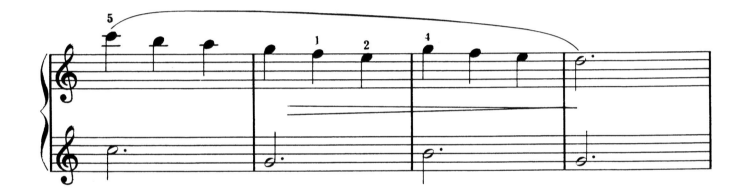

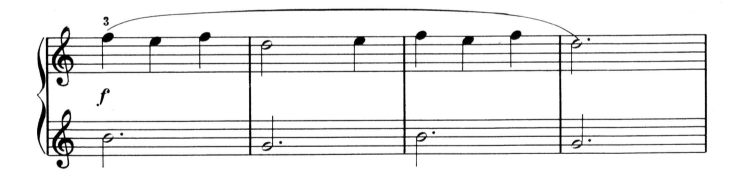

Secondo

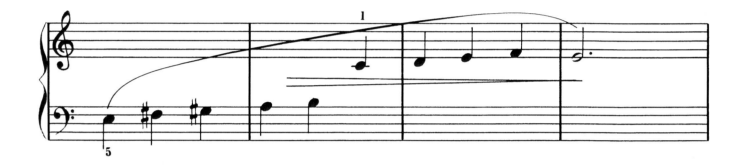

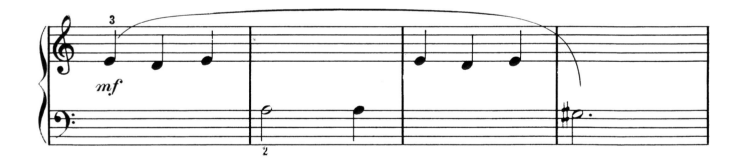

D.C. al Fine

Primo

D.C. al Fine

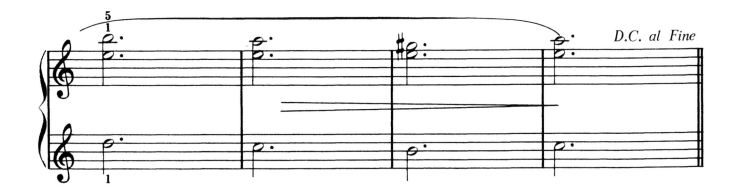

RICE PADDIES

RICE PADDIES

Primo

SWISS MUSIC BOX

Secondo

Lightly, with motion

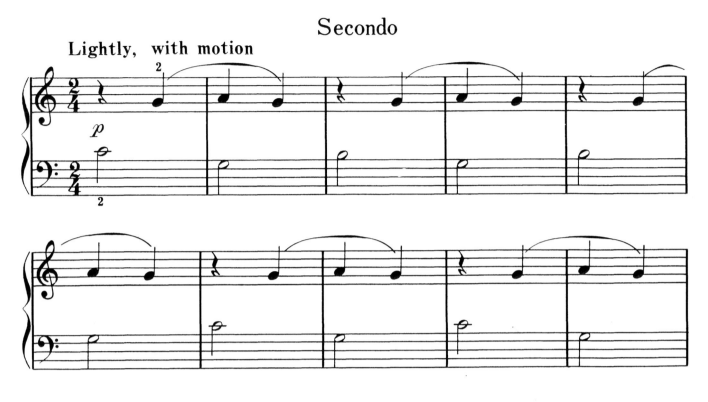

Fine

(poco a poco rit. 2nd time)

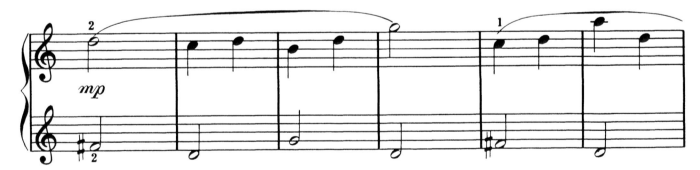

D.C. al Fine

SWISS MUSIC BOX

Primo

TICKER TOCKER

Secondo

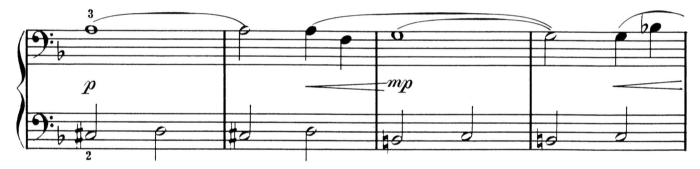

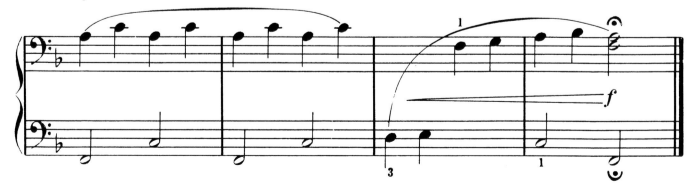

TICKER TOCKER

Primo

DUTCH TREAT

Secondo

DUTCH TREAT

Primo

Secondo

Primo

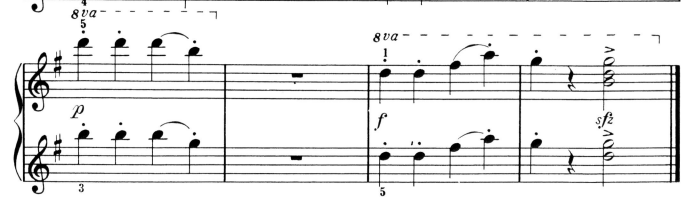